RADICAL EMBRACE

Francis Briers

Also by Francis Briers:

A Little Book on Finding your Way – Zen and the Art of Doing Stuff

Warrior Philosophy in Game of Thrones

The Little Book of Appreciation

My Tao Te Ching – A Fool's Guide to Effing the Ineffable

Editor:

The Embodiment Journal – Somatics and Embodiment for Health, Leadership, and Life

Contributed to:

The Compassionate Community: A Resource for Care Home Managers to Place Compassion at the Heart of Caring for Residents and Their Staff Teams (Frameworks 4change)

And coming soon...

Cultivating Wisdom: Why Wisdom is Being Lost and How We Can Save It

Radical Embrace:

Integrating Leadership, Embodiment, Compassion, and Sustainability

By Francis Briers

Warriors of Love Publishing

RADICAL EMBRACE

Copyright © Francis Briers 2015

The right of Francis Briers to be identified as the Author of the Work has been asserted by him in accordance with the Copyright, Designs and Patents Act 1988

All rights reserved. No part of this book may be used or reproduced in any manner whatsoever without written permission of the author except in the case of brief quotations embodied in articles and reviews. For more information contact Warriors of Love Publishing at www.fudoshin.org.uk

ISBN: 978-0-9567799-7-7

A copy of this book has been deposited with the British Library.

Published by Warriors of Love (WOL) Publishing

CONTENTS

1. Facing Reality: Feeling Overwhelmed # 7

2. Power: Will and the Urge to Lead # 31

3. Posture: Embodiment and Making a Stand for What You Believe In # 61

4. People: Competition, Collaboration, and Compassion # 83

5. Planet: Environment, Belonging and Legacy # 107

6. Conclusion: Dialogue + Action # 121

Resources # 129

Acknowledgements # 140

About the Author # 141

RADICAL EMBRACE

1

FACING REALITY:

FEELING OVERWHELMED

I frequently feel completely overwhelmed. When I look reality in the eye and honestly reflect on the state of the world around me I feel swamped. I can drown in the combination of the very real danger of environmental collapse, the hazardous imbalance of the current financial system both locally and globally, the all-too-often petty and self-serving political climate, the immediate challenge of keeping food on the table for my family, and the very real potential that I will burn myself out if I don't manage the pace of my work better. Facing all of that I feel totally overwhelmed and I'd be very surprised if I'm the only one. Optimist that I am (on a good day), I like to think that at least some of these challenges will shift and be addressed or resolved in the not-too-distant future. Obviously the smaller, more personal ones I have more control over but all of these difficulties on all of the levels feel to me so utterly interconnected that while I am earning a living today that could all come crashing down as a result of some aspect of the larger picture tomorrow. Looking after myself feels like a short-term solution, especially as I have a son and I don't want my legacy to my child to be a broken world, too far gone to repair.

Can you recognize this picture? My guess is that if you are reading this book then at least some of it will be ringing true for you too. I want to be clear early on that I don't have a magic bullet. I am no political, financial, or environmental expert here to offer you and the world a five-point-plan for fixing everything. What I do want to offer here is some of my thinking about how we can positively turn towards these many difficulties that lie before us rather than running away. I'm not judging that running away – it's a sane response to an insane world – but it's not going to shift the situation we find ourselves in. As I have been trying to make sense of the world, and my place in it, I have developed some ideas which I want to share with you for two basic reasons: firstly, out of compassion and in the hopes it may help you to feel less overwhelmed when looking modern life in the eye; secondly, because it is my conviction that if we don't all start taking a deep personal interest in taking care of our world then it may soon be too late. Many climate scientists say it already is too late, but I live in hope that if enough of us can mobilise effectively enough then maybe we can create a better future for our children. I'm certainly not convinced that some kind of super-hero leader is going to come and tell us all what to do and make it O.K. If we find solutions to our problems then I think it will come from a groundswell of concerned and caring individuals taking action and I'd like to be one of them. I hope you do too.

I am, in many ways, a creature of structure so here is the structure or model I have found useful in thinking about how I face this challenging world:

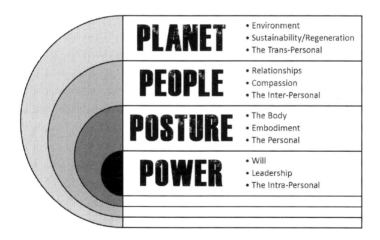

I am going to take a chapter on each of these 4 aspects so don't worry too much about the detail of what I mean by these words now, what might help to set it in context is looking at the flow from self to world. As well as finding structures or models like this useful in giving shape to my thinking, I also see structure as a useful metaphor in how we consider our approach. Different movements tend to emphasize different aspects of this flow but I believe that if we don't work through an integrated whole then our approach to our challenges will be structurally unsound and liable to collapse. This is one possible meaning of integrity: that the structure of our approach is sufficiently connected and coherent, the different aspects not just balanced but integrated with each other, that it becomes a strong whole rather than a combination of parts.

The first layer, the intra-personal, is about me relating internally with myself. This can happen through thinking, reflection, meditation and other internally focused processes. The second layer, the personal, is the bridge between this internal world and the outside world which I am seeing here primarily as the body. However, I am viewing the body through the lens of embodiment: as the subjective experience of my body as me, not the body as an object which I 'use.' The third layer, the interpersonal, is where I interact with other human beings through relationships. The fourth layer, the trans-personal, I am defining a little differently than its normal use. It is usually used to describe an awareness or sense of extending beyond (trans) the ordinary to encompass wider aspects of the psyche or the cosmos. The way I am using it here is not dissimilar but has a subtle distinction. I am using it to refer to our relationship with that which is greater than ourselves. This can include a concept of God, spirit, or the Divine if those aspects are meaningful to you but as you can probably guess from the fact that I have also labelled this layer 'Planet,' I am seeing the planet Earth as a being which is greater than us. I consider there to be literal truth to this in terms of viewing Earth as a huge organism, an integrated whole, as well as being made up of many disparate parts. There is also a spiritual aspect to this for me which comes from earth-based spiritual traditions whereby nature (the Earth) is seen as the visible face of spirit, and we as humans belong to the Earth rather than the

Earth belonging to us. I will explore this further in the chapter addressing this circle of concern but wanted to give you a basic sense of what I meant and how I am using the word 'trans-personal' in this context.

In many ways this model is not new. Ancient wisdom traditions such as Yoga, when you look at the whole system, had models or methods for integrated action which spanned the internal through the social, to the external world. However, many of these traditions have been only partially learned, passed on or practiced in their transition to the modern world. They also require a certain level of acceptance and commitment to the associated religious or spiritual beliefs. What I am seeking to do here is offer a model or way of seeing our choices for action in a manner which honours the wisdom of these ancient traditions while setting it in our modern context and, as far as possible, making it as accessible and free of specific belief-systems as I can.

Spiritual responses to the challenges we are facing in our world tend to be more focused on the inner circles, often the innermost domain of the intra-personal. The idea being that a primary cause of the problems in the world is a lack of consciousness. If we are operating from a more evolved consciousness then we will naturally take more responsibility for the impact we are having on the planet and each other and will spontaneously shift our behaviour. From this perspective it makes total sense to focus on the intra-personal, after all, only I can do the work to transform my consciousness. Only you can do the work to transform yours. As such I lead by example by doing the work to shift my consciousness and support others to do the same, thereby creating an impact in the interpersonal as an indirect consequence of my inner (intra-personal) work.

I think there is real validity in bringing fierce attention to the internal cultivation of consciousness; in fact I see it as a necessary aspect of our work if we are to really change the world. And... I don't think it's enough on its own. Don't get me wrong, I am not sitting here saying that all the Buddhist monks who are meditating hours every day to work towards enlightenment on behalf of all beings are wasting their time; I have long followed a spiritual path myself. We all have to make our own choices about how we fight the good fight. However, this is my philosophy and when I look at the world and for that matter when I look at myself, I can't stand back and work only internally. That's at least partially because I am not a monk - I have not retreated from the world to dedicate myself to a life of contemplation - I am in the world. I meet the world every day and I see my son growing up in it. I find in myself that I cannot stand by, that my own spiritual transformation must be, not only internally dedicated and in service, but must be linked to outer work.

The Activist is the role of those doing the outer work. They are out there rattling cages, shouting loud, directly challenging people and the organizational systems of our world to be different. They have a cause: people, animals, environment, disease, finance, there are so many causes. Part of my overwhelm when I look at the world is the sheer volume of causes people are seeking to rally around - I rarely see one which I don't instantly want to reach out on behalf of and help. But I can't help everyone and everything. Especially in the way that is so often asked - time, money, attention - all in finite supply. I can't help feeling that I just don't have enough to go around. I can't help feeling that I am somehow failing someone, some-being with every moment. Each time I see an advert for a charity or get accosted by a campaigner and fail to donate or sign up is another failure to help, another nail in the coffin of this precious world we live in. But again, I can't help everyone and everything; there is only so much of me to go around. How on Earth can I know what to do?

Not only do I have this struggle of knowing which path to take, which cause to lend my weight to, but what I see when I look at the world of activism is so often a dissonant picture. Some of the most overworked and stressed people I have met (and bear in mind that I sometimes teach stress management!) have been people doing the work of activism. The drive and passion for the cause can so often lead people to throw everything they have at the work they have chosen to do. Now, when I phrase it like that, it could sound like a good thing. After all, we live in a modern culture where "giving it your all," or "giving

150%," are attitudes towards work which are celebrated, but for me this is a mistake, especially when we are doing work which is about caring. If we are campaigning to get people and society to care for the planet, for animals, for a group of disadvantaged people, or to care more about our cause whatever that might be, then if we approach that campaign in such a way that we fail to care for ourselves, is that not hypocrisy? A lot of politicians and public figures get criticized in the press by campaigners for not practising what they preach. That's a much needed challenge and yet many of those same campaigners who vociferously advocate for the need to care about things which society seems to have forgotten, so often are not walking their talk in the subtle but important acts of their personal lives. The passion which drives them to speak out can also drive them to overwork themselves, which can often mean neglecting time with family and energy to nurture friendships too.

Just as I find I can't stand by, dedicated only to my spiritual work, equally I struggle to jump fully into the external battle of activism. How can we really do this work of caring for the world around us without sacrificing ourselves, and potentially those closest to us as well?

This then is my solution. I can't promise salvation for you, anyone or anything else, or this beautiful planet we inhabit. I don't have definitive answers about where we most need to use our finite resources to right the potentially sinking ship of humankind's survival on planet Earth. However, I can offer a framework; a guide to a way of being that is helping me to face into the difficulties and pain in the world rather than turning away from them. One thing is for sure: pretending nothing is wrong won't work. Numbing ourselves to the pain and distress in the world or living in denial will only narrow our window of opportunity for effective action. We may be facing more and greater challenges than ever before in human history and it is my conviction that we need to do something. So this philosophy, this framework, is my contribution. It is not another argument for a particular cause, it is a way of being. As well as offering a framework for certain kinds of action in and of itself it is also intended to help you to work out which are the battles you wish to engage in. I don't believe there is a single battle we can all lend our weight to and thereby resolve the difficulties we are facing. I wish there was. I wish such a simple conclusion was something I could offer you and myself but it's not. If we can all find a graceful way to turn towards the conflicts in the world and in ourselves, however, I believe we can also see clearly which battles are our battles. Perhaps, by taking our place in the bigger picture, the collective action on multiple fronts will make the difference needed to usher in the kind of planetary healing that is needed to build a better world for future generations.

A framework for understanding, knowing which are your battles and learning how to be part of a greater whole so we can act collectively: **This is Radical Embrace.**

We must have integrated action in ourselves, fully inhabiting our bodies, with each other, and in the world. We must embrace ourselves, each other and the world if we are to have the integrity to face the profound challenges of our time. We must take the radical and difficult step of really giving a shit. We need to find that place of absolute care and compassion deep down in ourselves and make the radical choice to bring the world, with all its pain and difficulty, closer to us. This embrace of the world cannot be limited to only the small, immediate picture of our own healing and development, or the big future picture of the world's healing and development but must be an embrace that starts within us and ripples outwards.

The framework I offered at the beginning is my expression of this Radical Embrace. We must embrace our own internal power to enable us to lead for change without losing sight of ourselves. We must embrace the oft-forgotten container of that power in this world, our bodies, microcosms of the world of matter and expression of the posture we adopt in relation to our lives. We must embrace each other as people, relinquishing the restrictions to our compassion of "us" and "them." And we must embrace the planet as a legitimate being rather than a resource to be used.

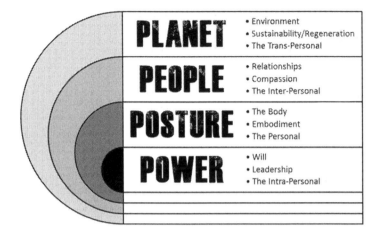

This model is made of circles of concern. It is my experience, and contention in this book, that if we get stuck in any one or just a couple of circles of concern then our engagement with our lives will be out of balance. The work of Radical Embrace is to make a full embrace of all these layers and integrate our circles of concern.

#

"Organisations move in the direction of the questions that we ask."

This is a quote associated with an organisational development philosophy called Appreciative Inquiry (AI) and I think it is no less true for individuals than organisations. If you ask questions about problems, you'll find problems. If you ask questions about strengths, you'll find strengths. The core idea behind AI is to find out what is working and then use that as a foundation, a place to stand from which we can build and grow. No matter how overwhelmed I might be, no matter how difficult the circumstances, there is always going to be something that is going well - some strength in me that I can build on. So, at the end of each chapter there is a key question designed to help you tap into your own gifts and wisdom in the area that the chapter has been exploring. These can just be questions you reflect on; they can be journaling questions which you make some time to write about as you go or after you have finished the book. They can also be dialogue questions to explore with your partner, a friend or a group of friends. The Buddha said that one of the three things needed to help people move towards enlightenment is 'Sangha' - a group of like-minded people. My friend and colleague Mark Walsh who is deeply expert when it comes to resilience says that generally as human beings "We are socially resilient." So another way to explore this work is to share this book with some friends and build a group of you who want to look at how you can practice and take action for a better world. Work with the ideas and areas of development here together instead of on your own and as part of this you can use the questions to shape your dialogue when you meet.

2

POWER:

WILL AND THE URGE TO LEAD

At this central layer, when I talk about the intra-personal, I mean your internal relationship with yourself. For many of us this inner relationship is one that plays out largely unconsciously. We have habits and conditioned ways of relating to ourselves which play out beneath the surface of our lives - all too often the invisible voice that is <u>really</u> telling us what to do. Carl Jung, one of the fathers of modern psychology said:

"Until we make the unconscious conscious it will rule our lives and we will call it fate."

The realm of the intra-personal is where this journey of making the unconscious conscious primarily happens. Through thinking, reflection, meditation, and other methods for gaining insight into our inner world we can understand ourselves better and make visible more of the forces which may be driving our behaviour. Values can be one aspect of this, the deep qualities which we consider to be most valuable in ourselves and others, the things for which we will stand up and be counted and which will significantly determine our friendships: sharing values creates bonds. Beliefs are another vital life-form in this domain, the underlying stories we tell ourselves about how the world works and our place in it. These can be broadly positive or negative in terms of whether they limit us or give us more freedom within ourselves, but even an ostensibly 'positive' belief can be limiting or even dangerous if it is blindly applied under the wrong circumstances. Believing that all people are basically good can be a wonderfully positive belief in meeting others until I meet someone who genuinely wishes me harm (for whatever reason) and then, if that belief is playing out unconsciously, I may ignore or be blind to the danger signals which could otherwise enable me to remove myself from a threatening situation. If we become conscious of our values we can more readily accept and appreciate those whose values differ from ours. If we become more conscious of our beliefs then we can challenge the beliefs that hold us back and be more careful in how we apply and follow all of our beliefs thereby being better able to meet the situations in our lives as they really are.

This realm of the intra-personal is the seat of our power. Our conscious choices begin from the inside out. It is in the theatre of this internal relationship with ourselves that our Will is shaped. Our Will defines our intentions, governs our direction, and determines our capacity for independence. Our

Will is the faculty responsible for our urge to lead. Whether or not we choose to make a stand for a cause and the determination with which we do so is a consequence of the shape and quality of our Will. The way we choose to influence others and create an impact in the world around us has its roots in the intra-personal dimension.

While a level of discipline and self-management is necessary for a child to function well in the world, all too often when a child's Will is developing it can be seen as an affront to the parent's power and then accordingly, is stamped on. This phase when the Will is gaining shape and momentum has in some subtle ways been demonised. Most people have heard of 'The Terrible Two's' and the majority of parents can identify with a sense of the challenge of parenting during the second and third years of their child's life. However, I believe that if a child's Will is too fiercely controlled or harshly stamped on in this first phase of its development then we potentially cripple our children's capacity for leadership - of themselves and others.

In Alfie Kohn's powerful book 'Unconditional Parenting' he talks about how the application of conditional and reward-based approaches to discipline destroy intrinsic motivation (where I do things because they feel good to me rather than because there is some external reward for doing so) and is driven by our need to control, not real care for the child's development. At this early age where rational thought and reasoned negotiation are so rare and inconsistent I can completely understand the desire to just find <u>some</u> way to get children to do as they are asked (or told). If we squash their Will though, or distort it so that there always needs to be a prize for them to be willing to pursue a goal, then we potentially damage their capacity for independent thought and action at a later stage - maybe for the rest of their lives.

Similarly, in her excellent book 'Lean In - Women, Work and the Will to Lead,' Sheryl Sandberg talks about being described as "Bossy" as a child and that this was a bad thing, a negative label. She particularly talks about it being applied to girls but I think these kinds of pejorative labels are another way that the Will can be squashed. While I understand completely the desire to help our children to learn to collaborate, often the drive to 'share' is pursued too fiercely, too early, when their brains have not yet developed the capacity to process the concept. I think the quality of leadership which can be so sought-after in adult life is rarely recognised as a potentially positive trait when it is strong in children and instead of helping them manage and socialise their wilfulness (Will-full-ness, to be full of Will), we seek to squash or deride it. The moniker "Bossy-Boots," is a common one, all-too-often used to shame a child into collaboration.

I have begun to wonder if we have a crisis of Will. I certainly think we have a crisis of leadership. I will say more about leadership shortly but in terms of Will, it seems to me that many if not most of our leaders are so driven by extrinsic reward that the idea of doing something because it is the right thing to do has almost become a ridiculous choice, something naive and archaic, particularly in senior business and political leadership. Whether it is about chasing approval or money, 'playing politics,' has become synonymous with dishonesty, selfishness, and manipulation. I think this is at least partially because we have, as a culture, become so chronically driven by the hoarding of external reward that for a leader's choices to be directed by anything other than their own selfish urge for gratification, or for a politician to do something just because they believe it's the right thing to do, is viewed with huge scepticism. Cynicism has become our default when it comes to leadership, and wilfulness has become associated with selfishness.

We need to reclaim our own Will, cultivate it in the next generation, and re-find our intrinsic motivation. The selfishness I have described above does not come from our true Will, it comes from conditioned habits of thought and motivation. If we can re-inhabit the space of our true Will then we can uncover what we really want in life, what is really important to us, rather than merely joining the habitual race to build the biggest pile of stuff. I think our true Will can be a compass helping us to intuitively stay on track, moving through life with purpose, passion and conviction.

I think part of what has created our cynicism about leadership is actually a deeper desire for truly great leadership. The irony is that the cynicism makes it very unlikely we would accept such a leader even if one came along.

I would say that the current prevailing model of leadership is still 'Heroic Leadership,' whereby we see a leader as someone who stands up in front of us and says "I know the answer, I know what to do, follow me!" We may have highly sophisticated theoretical models of leadership and this is not to say that some people aren't exploring and practicing leadership in other ways but, culturally, the heroic stance is still something we expect to see. More than that expectation, in the face of the massive complexity of the modern world with the many immense challenges facing us politically, ecologically, socially, technologically, on pretty much every level, I think deep down we would all breathe a huge sigh of relief if someone stood up and convincingly said "I know what to do." I don't believe the sense of overwhelm I described at the beginning of this book is unique to me: it's understandable that we would want someone to step in and rescue us from our struggles, pain and discomfort. However, even if such a leader existed I think they would be hamstrung by our political systems and hung out to dry by our media.

Our political systems are mostly not set up to let a single leader decisively run things and generally speaking, that's a good thing. The party political system means, particularly in the UK and America and I'd suggest in most democratically run countries this will be echoed, that the nominal leader is dependent for the really big changes on gaining consensus or at least substantial support from many other people including those not under their direct party leadership. In terms of the media, the most common pattern we see with leaders if they are given any credit at all is that they are raised up as Gods and then torn down for disappointing us.

Obama is a great example of these dynamics. I can remember for myself the huge surge of hope and the sense of possibility around his election. Here was a man who might really be able to change things, the leader of arguably the most powerful single nation in the world and he seemed to have real vision. Then, so much of what he has sought to do that would have been truly transformational has been blocked or crippled by the Senate or Congress and the world media has writ large his failure to perform the miracles we expected from him.

This seems to me to be the game we collectively play with ourselves around leadership: we set them up, and then knock them down. The child in us gets carried away by the story of hope embodied in the latest hero, then the jaded adult in us colludes in creating the story of their failure thereby validating that jaded adult in the habitually cynical position we have learned to adopt. What leader <u>could</u> succeed in such a toxic system?!

My suspicion is that the Heroic model of leadership is broken. I think historically it has functioned when leaders have been able to define a single, clear enemy against whom we can unite but we are unlikely to see such a clear-cut situation again. Between the sheer complexity and scale of the challenges facing us, their impersonal nature (it's not so much a group of people as complex systemic social, political, and environmental issues), and the contrariness of the press in raising people up as Gods and denouncing them as demons, how would such a heroic leader ever emerge? However, even if one did, I'm not convinced that it is necessarily the most effective model of leadership anyway. Especially in an age where the potential to form highly coordinated, distributed leadership is more possible than ever. The quality of our communications and the tools at our disposal make it more possible than ever before to have leadership be run on the 'think globally, act locally' principle. I'd suggest we need some kind of global coordination of efforts but for that to be made up of many local leaders. To make that possible we need to stop chasing heroes.

We each need to look after the frightened child inside our selves rather than looking for an external saviour to do it for us. I think the jaded, cynical adult psyche needs healing and releasing. Perhaps, if we can integrate these two aspects of ourselves, the helpless innocent and the hopeless cynic, we can find a more balanced position of true maturity from which we can take wise, maybe cautious, but essentially hopeful action.

If we let hope die then effective action will be the next casualty, because hopelessness breeds resignation and abdication.

We need to stop chasing hero's and build networks. We need to let go of the myth that someone will make the best choices for us and exercise wise and compassionate choice for ourselves, each other, and the planet.

If we are going to stop looking to others for all our leadership needs then we must become more skilful at leadership ourselves. There are lots of myths about leadership, one of which is that leaders are born, not made, and not everyone can be a leader. As you will come to see, I consider leadership to be a foundational human capacity which we can develop and become skilful at wielding, not a 'special' talent which you either have or you don't. Just like any other skill, some people have a natural talent which gives them a head-start in some ways, but anyone can work at it and become skilful. For sure, the best in the world are probably talented and skilful, but if we are to create this network of distributed leadership I have mentioned we must all be ready to take responsibility and embrace leadership where it is needed.

There are many definitions of leadership in the field. I'm not going to argue for one being right and others being wrong. The most functionally useful one I have found, however is as follows:

"A leader is anyone who influences others to take effective action."[1]

When a baby cries and its mother picks it up, who is the leader? The baby! We are literally exercising leadership from the cradle. In fact I would

---

[1] This definition is taken from the Cadet's Handbook for West Point Military Academy in the U.S. The same section of definition also distinguishes between leadership and two other functions: Management - which is about optimising use of resources and implementing process, and Command (being the Boss) which is about a position in the organisation whereby there is a consequence for your orders not being followed. Whether you like or believe in what military organisations stand for, they have been formally studying leadership probably for longer than anyone else and their conclusions have been well tested.

suggest that we are exercising our leadership all the time, whether we realise it or not. We cannot help but influence those around us; even failure to act or actively choose is a choice by abdication. The difference then becomes whether we actively engage with our power to lead or passively and perhaps unconsciously influence the world around us by default.

Even though leadership is such a fundamental aspect of human nature, most people will not have spent much time studying it or developing skill with it. Unless you have a job managing a team it's unlikely you will have spent much time, if any developing your leadership. Managers, on the other hand, are likely to receive leadership training of some kind and the more senior you get, the more training and development you are likely to be given. In this way, the corporate world in particular has been creating an educational elite: a group of people who are likely to have had far more education and training than most other people, and much of that training will have focused on leadership in some way.

It could be easy to look at this situation around leadership development and say "Well, I don't lead anyone anyway, maybe I don't need it." But I would contend that leadership begins with self-leadership. Leadership development is at least partially development of your Will, the faculty which gives you a sense of direction and purpose, the human aspect most involved in making powerful choices. A conspiracy theorist might look at this and spot that if you want to make sure people remain passive and easy to tell what to do, make sure they never realise that they are themselves, leaders. I'm not convinced there is anything particularly Machiavellian going on here. I think this is more of an error by omission: the corporate and more broadly organisational world and society even more generally, just assuming that if you don't obviously have people to lead then why invest in leadership training?

Leadership development when offered more generally can be a deeply radical act. Helping people to learn how to lead themselves, to develop their Will, to make powerful choices, to have a greater sense of meaning and purpose in their lives, is the stuff of awakening and lays the groundwork for revolution.

I would hope for that revolution to be a compassionate one where people who have realised their own power to choose begin to coordinate and choose differently, rebuilding by redirection of energy and focus rather than by destruction (thereby forcing rebuilding). Nonetheless I think we need some kind of profound change if we are not to find ourselves fast becoming extinct. This is why I consider Will and leadership to be one of the four foundations of what I have come to call Radical Embrace. Leadership is about embracing our own power and growing our capacity to wield it wisely. This is why you will find me addressing questions of leadership with pretty much every group of people I work with as a facilitator and trainer, regardless of whether they consider themselves leaders. I consider leadership to be a foundational human capacity - we are influencing each other all the time whether we like it or not - the questions then become:

Are we influencing each other to take effective action or passively leading each other off a metaphorical cliff?

And ...What then do we consider effective?

My hope is that the rest of this book may help you to consider these questions. We all have to answer them for ourselves and I'll be honest with you, my agenda here is to exercise my leadership: to compassionately influence you to take effective action. We need a network of distributed leadership where many different people are making a stand for many different important issues and gather the support they need to really make a difference. This framework I am offering then is about working out for yourself what you will stand up and be counted for. In service of that then, here is the first of the big questions I'm inviting you to consider to shape your own path of Radical Embrace:

"What do you care so much about that you will put your leadership in service to it?"

Leadership requires courage, daring, and a willingness to be visible in your care. I sometimes extend the first working definition of leadership I have offered to become:

A leader at their best is someone who inspires others to courageous action.

I think we still need to consider what 'effective' looks like in this context as courage can be wielded foolishly but this extension brings in the idea of inspiration as a way of influence and highlights the fact that leadership requires courage to embrace. Combine this with what Ralph Nader said about leadership:

"The function of leadership is to produce more leaders, not more followers."

And we have a pretty good foundation for the kind of wise leadership I'd love to see more people embrace. So, to link with the next section, what will you make a stand for? What is so important to you that it ceases to be an egotistical drive for you to lead it? So the move into leadership becomes natural for you, almost unthinking, and you welcome others in that space too because it's so important you just want to see this thing rise up and fly. What cause can you surrender yourself to?

There can be a discomfort for people around the ideas of leadership and power. In some circles they have become dirty words - and understandably so, as they are both capacities which are frequently misused in service to someone's ego and wish to control others. I don't consider that true leadership as, in the wider context, it is not effective and I think we need to reclaim power as the blessing it can be.

We must reclaim power and leadership as sacred gifts. That doesn't require any religious beliefs. Sacredness has to do with something being so precious that we treat it with reverence and deep respect. So if you take the first scary step and admit to yourself that you care deeply about the world, what then is at the heart of that care? What cause sings to your soul so clearly that you cannot help yourself but stand up and

offer these sacred gifts for its sake?

For the sake of

what will you

embrace your power

to lead?

3

POSTURE:

EMBODIMENT AND MAKING A STAND FOR WHAT YOU BELIEVE IN

Having begun with the intra-personal often people will then move to talking about the interpersonal: relationships. This is very reasonable in many ways; one is the inner sense of relationship, the other the outer sense of relationship. Inside, outside. However, I think this misses out reflecting on the bridge between, the container of the intra-personal and the medium of the interpersonal. Here I am seeing that bridge as being the body and, as I will shortly describe, the body often gets missed out or underestimated in this way.

I want to take a moment to speak a little about the domain of the Personal before I circle back to the body. I have begun to wonder if our seemingly habitual missing out of the Personal in our consideration of ourselves is part of our problem. "Don't take it personally" is a phrase you will often hear people say and I understand its meaning and value in the way it is usually used. It can be helpful to not take things personally, to maintain a sense of perspective, but I think that if we are to truly stand up and look the world's greatest challenges in the eye we have to start <u>taking it personally</u>. We must start getting personally upset about the cruelty being perpetrated against people and the planet - upset enough to do something about it.

Anger as an emotion often gets a bad rap but it is an emotion that lets us know that we believe something bad has happened to someone or something we care about. When Bob Geldof made LiveAid happen I think he was fuelled significantly by anger. I remember seeing him talking about it on the news and he was furious about what was happening in Africa: Furious enough to do something about it. The trick is to find our passion and fire to fuel us to take action while maintaining sufficient capacity for calmness and grace that we can ensure our action is effective. While anger can be positive, it doesn't have a bad rap for nothing - it can be part of a physiological process which compromises our ability for clear rational action and reasoned choice[2].

Managing our state in our body is for many people an underdeveloped skill but the good news is that it can be learned, and it is one of the keys to having our emotions without them robbing us of our capacity for reasoned thought. The body seems particularly pertinent when we look at how we can learn to constructively 'take things personally.'

---

[2] Emotional Intelligence @ Work – Jolyon Maddocks, Chapter 2

In essence, I think that our ignoring of the Personal is a way we habitually avoid responsibility.

If we reflect primarily on the intrapersonal we can focus mainly on how our past has shaped our psychology - and it is therefore not really our fault, the world made us this way. If we reflect mainly on the interpersonal then we can talk lots about relationship and the other people involved and even if we own some of the responsibility in this realm, there are many factors involved: <u>we</u> can't be held responsible for all of it. So this invitation into the unusual step of reflecting on the Personal, the bridge between intra and inter, is a step into taking responsibility as well. There are no excuses, here, it's all you. The bad news is that we all have a part in what we have created in the world; the good news is that we all have the power to choose differently.

#

We live in a disembodied world. Obviously that is a pretty cut-and-dried statement and it's not quite that clear cut but it's not far off. The prevailing culture in the vast majority of the modern world is one which demotes, discourages, devalues, and even demonizes the body and, as far as I can see, that is only getting worse.

You could point to professional sport or the body beautiful (models, actors, actresses), or gym and fitness culture as examples of the primacy of the body in the modern world: surely these are places where the body is valued? I would suggest not. In my assessment, for the body to truly be valued it must be embraced as me, myself, the home of my physical identity in this world. The disciplines and environments mentioned above, for the most part, don't hold the body in this regard.

Professional sport tends to treat the body as a high performance machine to be continuously fine-tuned for peak-performance in the short period of its physical prime. Athletes are well known for having serious physical difficulties later on in life as a consequence of the punishing regimes they adhere to in order to get the edge in competition.

The various places focused on 'the body beautiful' treat the body as an artwork, an aesthetic medium to be sculpted, moulded, decorated - even deceptively, after the fact, through air-brushing of images and digital manipulation. Some elements of the body are emphasised, others hidden, driven by a mythical aesthetic ideal of what 'beautiful' really looks like. Models are well known for frequently suffering with eating disorders, body-builders for taking steroids, actors and actresses for various kinds of psychological distress and addictions.

Gym and fitness culture tends to be a subtler blend of these two previous environments where the body is a thing to be "made" fitter, more shapely or 'buff.' People talk in glowing terms about classes and instructors where they are being 'knocked into shape,' or smilingly declare a session as 'punishing.' So much of the language in fitness culture treats the body as an enemy to be conquered and controlled - this is not a relationship of love and respect but one of superiority and distrust.

    The environments I have mentioned above are not inherently bad. I love witnessing the incredible feats of athletes in their prime. I used to be an actor myself and really enjoy the amazing beauty, handsomeness, and at times almost unearthly elegance of actors, actresses and models - it can all be amazing art. I see that many people enjoy and benefit from getting fit in various ways and with office jobs where we are physically inactive so much of the time things like gyms become necessary for health. What I find both sad and deeply concerning is the attitude which exists within the culture of these environments whereby the body is treated as an object, a thing, even an opponent. The body is not typically respected, listened to, or loved.

Many people disparagingly criticize the cultural tendency to objectify women's bodies in advertising and the media. That's a totally valid position, but people espousing it rarely seem to realise that most people objectify their own and each other's bodies as a matter of course. Objectification is an epidemic, not an attitude limited to advertisers using scantily-clad women to sell things.

#

Embodiment is the radical act of embracing the body as me, home to my spirit, in fact indivisible from any other part of me. Such separation is an illusion: each of us is an integrated whole and this aspect we call a body is an element within a wonderful, interconnected system. The body is not an 'it,' thing, object, or machine. The brain is not the boss, in fact so much of the wider nervous system sits in the 'rest' of the body and cognition is so interconnected with physical action that we could even argue that the body <u>is</u> the brain.

Again: all parts of an integrated whole.

"Embodiment," as my friend and colleague Mark Walsh says, "is how you are." We are all practicing things in every moment and whatever we practice shapes our thinking, feeling, seeing, indeed our entire being. If I walk or stand a certain way, if I repeat a certain gesture, if I adopt a certain tension repeatedly, if I have an injury and my body begins to compensate for the pain through subtly adjusting my posture, whatever I am doing in my body shapes who I am - and this is embodiment. The collection of physical patterns and actions, the million subtle things I am practicing in each moment, this is the good-news and the bad-news about myself: this is what we call my personality. Embodiment isn't about body shape or type, it is not about aesthetics or athletics, it is about how I inhabit my body.

My embodiment shapes who I am, how I am, how I see the world, and even what is possible for me ...

... not just physically but mentally, emotionally, and arguably spiritually as well.

Disembodiment does not stop any of this being the case it just means that we are passive victims of whatever bodily forces are shaping us. We take a stance to the world and this becomes an entrenched way of acting, thinking, feeling and being. I get injured and the many ways my body compensates for the changes in structure, strength and balance subtly twists my world-view. I lift weights at the gym and as I isolate and harden my muscles I isolate and harden myself. I slump and collapse in my posture and then experience an emotional slump as well. Just like our fears about subliminal advertising, something is unconsciously shaping our behaviour without our permission or awareness... Our relationship with our bodies.

One of the costs of disembodiment is this unconscious shaping of our thoughts, emotions, and mood. When we engage with embodiment we potentially gain - at least - much more awareness, and hopefully more choice about our way of being moment-to-moment.

Another cost of disembodiment is that by treating ourselves in a certain way we develop habits which we will apply to others as well.[3] Therefore if, as I have described here, we objectify our own bodies, we are more likely to objectify other people too. They become a 'thing' in space and are therefore easier to use, mistreat, or discard.

Our relationship with our bodies is connected with the 'big body' of Mother Earth. If we engage with embodiment and mindfully inhabit our bodies as fully integrated aspects of a holistic self then we set the

---

[3] In one piece of research with psychotherapists in the US the researchers mapped out the therapists internal dialogue – the way they 'talked' to themselves. They then analysed how these same therapists spoke to their clients, the kinds of conversations they had. There was (perhaps unsurprisingly) a strong correlation between critical self-talk and being critical with clients. http://psycnet.apa.org/psycinfo/1991-10561-001

conditions for relating to the planet in a mindful and loving way. By objectifying our bodies we create the conditions in our psyche's whereby we will objectify the world. Self-objectification is then linked to how we see the planet as a 'resource' to be 'used' instead of a dynamic and complex organic system to be treated with respect and reverence. By engaging with embodiment, by radically embracing and respecting our bodies, we can lay the foundations in ourselves to treat other people, animals, indeed the whole world with greater dignity and respect. Compassion, mindfulness, and responsible action begin in the body.

#

As I have said, Embodiment is how you are.

The posture I adopt is shaped by, and shapes both my experience of the world and the way the rest of the world experiences me.

We commonly talk in philosophical or political terms about "making a stand" for something, or "standing up for what you believe in," or "taking a stance" towards an issue. These phrases are not just metaphorical when seen through this lens of embodiment, they are literal. Your attitude towards life, your embodied philosophy is created by and expressed through the stance, the posture you take towards the world every moment. The good news is that you can change it, you can literally shape it through practicing a different posture and way of moving.

What stance do you want to take towards the world? What do you want to embody? Essentially: Who do you want to be?

Traditional psychology wielded unskilfully has the potential to make victims of us by telling the story that 'who I am' is the consequence of the many things that have happened <u>to</u> me through the history of my life. It's not that this doesn't have some truth in it, but we can also take responsibility for our future and say "Who do I want to be and how do I create myself that way?" We can accept our past history and then take responsibility for shaping our future rather than blaming our past for the mess that is coming around the corner.

#

One way to define responsibility is to break it down: Respond-ability, or the ability to respond rather than just have a knee-jerk reaction. This isn't to say that everything is your fault! Any idea of blame in fact goes against the idea of responsibility and if we lay blame at our own door then we victimize ourselves. Responsibility is about recognizing and taking ownership of what we <u>can</u> do <u>in the face of</u> what life throws at us[4]. If I wield the idea of responsibility

---

[4] If you want to read more on this approach to the idea of responsibility, Viktor Frankl is in many ways one of the greatest exponents of this philosophy in the modern world. Fred Kofman also writes eloquently about its application in working life.

clumsily then I can end up making it my fault that it rains! I can't control if it rains but I can choose how I dress or whether or not I carry an umbrella. This isn't about becoming some kind of boy-scout extremist, prepared for any eventuality, it is about recognizing that when I get wet the rain is only part of the picture - I chose to go out, I misjudged the weather and didn't wear water-proofs etc. I am partially responsible. The same is true when multiple people are involved in a situation: Usually everyone involved will be at least partially responsible even if only due to their tolerance or inaction in the face of a difficult circumstance.

If I am to take responsibility for my life and the world that I live in, I need to say to myself: "I am part of the system that has created this mess, I am partly responsible here, what am I going to do about it?" The cost of responsibility is that I can no-longer stand on the side-lines and paint myself as an innocent while I decide who is to blame. The pay-off is that I empower myself to make a stand and take action. To create a different outcome in the future.

To bring us full-circle in this chapter, we can combine taking things personally and taking responsibility to shape our choices about the stand we want to make in the world - what posture we want to adopt. The question then for this chapter is:

What are you creating, each moment, through your presence?

4

PEOPLE:

COMPETITION, COLLABORATION, AND COMPASSION

The interpersonal is probably a realm you are used to hearing about. It is probably more familiar territory than the intra-personal or the personal. The interpersonal is the realm of relationships. This is where we play out some of those underlying and unconscious stories about ourselves and the world in the ways we relate to each other, in the ways we form intimate relationships and how we form the broader relationships we have with groups of people. This is how we form a sense of belonging or 'Tribe.'

The way we form our relationships hugely influences how we live our lives. The people we surround ourselves with will shape us just as we shape them. Groups of people build group identities which, while they are originally built by the group of individuals involved then have a life of their own to some extent and feed back into the lives and personalities of those individuals. We tend to become more like the people we spend time with. The subtle rhythms in our bodies will tend to synch with each other through the process of entrainment[5], our emotional landscapes will influence each other, becoming increasingly similar. The stories we tell ourselves about the way the world works will be shared through our conversations - sometimes directly and explicitly, sometimes subtly through our attitudes. Eventually we will have many of our internal stories in common and the way we see the world, the beliefs we hold about reality, will be common too[6].

Often when we try to make changes in our lives, our friends and family can be part of a system of resistance rather than support. This isn't always the

---

[5] For more on this see 'The Silent Pulse' by George Leonard, and 'Timeshifting' by Stephan Rechtschaffen

[6] This perspective is central to the sociological school of thought 'Social Construction' which was a big influence on the formation of Appreciative Inquiry – the method which inspired the questions I ask in the book

case but due to our identities becoming so enmeshed with each other in the ways I have described, if we make changes, that threatens the identity of the group and in evolutionary terms that shared group identity was part of what kept us safe. We are pack animals and individual psychological changes threaten the integrity of the group. This is part of what drives group-think, peer pressure, and other forms of suppression of individual choice by 'tribes' of people. Belonging is a primal need for us as a species and if your choices seem to threaten that shared state of belonging you can transform from friend to foe.

Conversely, our communities can be the very thing which enables us to achieve our greatest feats. As I mentioned in the first chapter, my friend and colleague Mark Walsh says "we are socially resilient." Our relationships enable us to survive and bounce back in tough times, and those who surround us can inspire us and support us to make the transition from one way of being to another. When we face our toughest challenges one of the key questions that a therapist will ask is "Do you have a network of support?" I think many pastimes and hobbies are as driven by a desire to find a group of like-minded people as they are by a love of the activities themselves.

    I'm sure you can see, the drive to belong can be an enabling or disabling factor. It shapes how we relate to the world and can be a source of personal strength or a fragile thing needing protection. It can be a source of peace or a cause for conflict.

RADICAL EMBRACE

The smallest tribe I can belong to is the tribe within. This is equivalent to the intra-personal in the framework I have been describing - the different aspects of myself, the different voices inside me. When I talk about 'voices' I am not referring to multiple personalities such as would be found in mental illness. From one point of view we all have multiple voices within us. The therapeutic method 'Voice Dialogue'[7] is based on this idea - that we can listen to the different aspects and attitudes that sometimes war within us as separate voices. Even someone totally isolated, or someone who seems to hate themselves will still belong to this inner tribe, and there will still exist voices of support though they may be quiet.

---

[7] Embracing Our Selves – The Voice Dialogue Manual by Hal Stone

The next biggest tribe is the tribe of me on the outside: The idea of the lone wolf which, as you may have guessed, aligns with what I describe here as the personal. This is the home of the idea that I belong to myself, the rugged individualist, the self-dependent, pull myself up by my bootstraps, entrepreneur, self-made-man (or woman). In the modern Western world, even those who belong to larger groups often have a strong sense of this. The individualism particularly prevalent in the U.S. but also strong in the U.K. and parts of Europe creates powerfully independent people but also isolates us. Sociologists and politicians talk about the breakdown of the family unit and come up with many reasons why that is happening but for me it is this philosophical stance which is most likely responsible. If I belong to myself then I am responsible only for myself.

The next biggest tribe is of course a tribe with others. However, we can break this down in different ways. Fred Kofman[8] describes something similar to what I am setting out here.

Kofman begins, like me, with only caring about myself, my own needs. This is a normal stage of development in children who will seem to act 'selfishly' but they don't yet have the capacity to really be concerned for the other person's feelings. In the moment of wanting they can only identify what they want without really understanding the impact for others. As Kofman puts it "This is fine at five but quite

---

[8] In his book 'Conscious Business,' Chapter 9, P276-277

problematic at twenty-five," and yet some people are stuck in this level of development. In fact I would suggest that the myth of the rugged individualist, the lone wolf, has kept many of us stuck in some place in our psyches at this child-level of development. What many see as being mature, rational (if perhaps coldly so), is actually not mature at all. It is a playing out of this very early stage of development: Me first and hang the rest. Kofman calls this "Egocentric."

The next stage Kofman describes is "Ethnocentric," which is all about 'us.' In this level I have learned to care about others but that is limited. As Kofman writes, at this level I only care about the needs of those with whom I belong. If you are not 'one of us' then your needs are not important. This sense of concern extends to the family, the clan, the tribe, the nation, the race - whatever group I feel attached to - but anyone who doesn't belong to that group is not worthy of my concern. Even murderers may take great care of their family or friends. Kofman shares a very pertinent quote from philosopher Ken Wilber: "Nazis loved their children."

The next stage is "World-centric" which is about all of us. The exclusivity of care seen at the ethnocentric level has fallen away so that if I am operating at this level of development I care about all of humanity and embody a universal set of values which can seem quite abstract. The sense of care, however, is concrete and the attitude of 'us-vs.-them' has been relinquished.

Hopefully you can see that when we consider the inter-personal it is vital to look at which level we are focused on. I don't see these levels only as levels of development but as layers of focus too. I have met plenty of people who seem very able to embody deep care and concern for all of humanity but are not taking good care of themselves in some way. That is why I see this framework of Radical Embrace as a model for integration not linear development: To have a healthy expansion of our sense of care and concern, that needs to rest on a very solid foundation of self-care. To be able to healthily embrace the world we must first embrace ourselves. This self-care must be in service to our community and something bigger than us though, if it is not to become narcissism.

I think it is healthy for us as human-beings to have tribes. We gain a sense of belonging, closeness, and support from finding those with whom we have most in common and spending time together. As I touched on earlier, The Buddha said that the three things required to achieve enlightenment were Dharma - the teachings, Buddha - contact with your own enlightened nature (through meditation perhaps), and Sangha - a group of like-minded, like-hearted people. Even in seeking total transcendence of all boundaries and illusions of separation Buddha didn't say "it doesn't matter who is around you, you **should** be able to love everyone." We are all works-in-progress and we all need support from our nearest-and-dearest sometimes. The important thing is to not be limited by our tribes, to not get stuck at that level of development as Kofman frames it. We need to grow our capacity to care just because we are faced with another human-being: another work-in-progress who may need our support, even if only for a moment. We need to care beyond self, family, tribe, and nation. We need to learn to care just because we can.

#

People often equate competition with a lack of compassion or care, and seek to replace it with collaboration but I think both are necessary. Competition doesn't need to be ruthless. One way of viewing the classical relationship of Yin and Yang as opposites is that, although they have opposite qualities, each contains a seed of the other and they are in fact mutually nourishing and supporting - indeed, one can't exist without the other. I see competition and collaboration in this light: they seem like opposites but they actually nourish and support each other. Collaboration is often called forth most powerfully when people are seeking to take collective action in the face of fierce competition. Even more essentially, any competition which stops short of total annihilation of one's opponent as the goal, necessarily has to involve collaboration.

Consider a football (soccer) match. Under normal circumstances if I walked onto the pitch armed with a gun I could achieve the aim of scoring more goals than the other team relatively easily - I win! However, we know that even in the most hard-fought competitions in the world, even when the teams dislike each other, they stop short of carrying weapons. Collaboration is at play here! Obviously this is an extreme example to illustrate the case but hopefully you can see from this that even when we think we are at our most competitive, we are still collaborating too. Most people would also agree that the best sports competitions occur when the competitors (teams or individuals) are 'playing fair' - or to put it another way, being most collaborative.

When we learn to see competition in this light, as an honourable, dignified and collaborative pursuit, we open the door to competition being an act of profound intimacy where we bring out the best in each other. We let go of the distasteful rhetoric of 'destroying' our opponents and I seek to bring my best game because to do less would be disrespectful of your talents and effort, while also wishing you to bring your best game because otherwise what is the point? The outcome of the activity is an integral part of the competitive experience but ceases to be the primary focus of our attention.

When we learn to see collaboration in this light - as a fierce, playful, challenging environment - we open the door to collaboration being a passionate embrace of each other and the challenges we face. We can let go of the need to 'play nice' and can be more rigorously honest, pushing our edges to bring out the best in each other and to find the best solutions.

Here we see yet another way that it is easy for us to culturally polarise, to make some people part of our tribe and 'good,' and other people outside our tribe and 'bad.' This kind of divisiveness, buried so deep in our human natures, may in some ways be our greatest challenge to resolving the huge and potentially catastrophic problems which are playing out on the world stage.

Can we integrate competition and collaboration so we can mobilise, excel, and care for each other enough to solve the world's greatest difficulties?

As far as I can see compassion is a capacity which is fast becoming a dire necessity. Many people see it as innate "You either have it or you don't" is a phrase I have heard a lot in extensive work I have done sharing practices to cultivate compassion in health and social care environments. However, I think that any faculty we have as human beings can be consciously cultivated, short of there being some psychological or physiological barrier to that development. Both my experience and the research I have done in the field of human potential suggest this is true.

The current leading edge research tells us that compassion can be cultivated.

Studies have been conducted in the US which have showed measurable changes in brain activity[9] and clear results in psychological studies[10] which suggest that compassion (and similar qualities such as altruism) can be taught, developed, and grown. When we are facing a world so full of challenges and conflict, why wouldn't we invest some time in cultivating greater compassion?

Really, the state of compassion is at the heart of all relationships. We either choose to help others or choose to leave them stranded, because of a felt sense

---

[9] 'Compassion Training Alters Altruism and Neural Responses to Suffering' – Psychological Science, May 2013 – Helen Weng lead author

[10] 'Promoting Altruism Through Meditation: An 8-Week Randomized Controlled Pilot Study' - Mindfulness, September 2013, Volume 4, Issue 3

of compassion. The Latinate root of the word has 2 parts which when put together translate as 'to suffer with' and therein lies the true challenge: are we willing to keep reaching out, to keep connected with each other as fellow human-beings in the face of suffering or do we attempt to choose those who will survive and sacrifice the rest? Are we willing to let the suffering of others in enough that their pain becomes our pain, and we can't help but do something to reach out and help? Can we do this without deifying collaboration and demonising competition? These are big questions, but while there are those special souls who automatically jump into the breach to assist others regardless of the risks to themselves, we are not all wired like that. Most of us need to ***practice*** offering our compassion and work on expanding our circle of concern to include the greater world. I would suggest that it is better to offer deep compassion in a small area than to rush out and overwhelm ourselves with the great cry of the world where so many people are in such deep need. We need to open ourselves to expressing compassion beyond our immediate circle, but if we all offered real care to those we most immediately come into contact with, the ripples of that care would echo out. From this way of moving through the world, we would naturally create communities and systems within which compassion is expressed, collaboration flourishes, competition is nourishing and respectful, and needs get met.

To begin in your immediate environment, your family or tribe and the many random people who cross your path every day, here's a question to reflect on:

What is the impact you are making on the lives of those around you?

RADICAL EMBRACE

5

PLANET:

ENVIRONMENT, BELONGING, AND LEGACY

For me, the Trans-personal is about our relationship with that-which-is-greater-than-us. This is a deliberately broad description which includes but is not limited to ideas of Divinity, Spirit, God or Love as a living principle.

In the previous chapter I described several different stages of development as laid out by Fred Kofman. The final one he describes is "Spirit-centric" where a person develops the awareness to have care and concern for all sentient life. I want to be clear that for me this includes the planet Earth, the whole environment in which we live. In many indigenous and earth-based spiritual traditions nature is seen as 'the visible face of spirit,' and that is what I am talking about here. Spirit or God doesn't need to be a distant or theoretical concept. For some people of faith this wouldn't be true anyway but whether you are obviously religious or spiritual or not, in my view, there is a solid and very real being-greater-than-us right beneath our feet and all around us every minute. The trans-personal doesn't have to mean transcendence into some other spiritual realm, it can mean transcending our small, personal concerns to acknowledge the planet Earth as a legitimate being. A being which gives us life and therefore is justifiably called 'Mother.'

For most of us in the modern world we relate to the planet, to our environment as something which can be owned and used as a resource. Again, a difference which we can learn from many of the ancient indigenous cultures is relating to the Earth through a sense of belonging rather than ownership. A phrase I have heard in various indigenous traditions is "We belong to the Land," rather than the modern convention of "The land belongs to me." I see much to be learned from indigenous traditions and teachings and I don't see our development as human beings as having been entirely linear, past-to-future. I don't wish to romanticize the past as a kind of tribal golden-age but there is much the ancient world can teach us to help with our modern lives.

    My hope here is to take the trans-personal and make it solid enough that whatever your religious or spiritual orientation you can expand your circle of concern to include this layer of awareness and the great, bright and beautiful being that is Mother Earth. Whatever your spiritual beliefs, the Earth is definitely there and definitely needs our care and attention, just as it supports and nourishes us in every moment.

#

"Sustainability," is the current primary language of care for the Earth but some friends[11] introduced me to a concept which seems infinitely richer: Regeneration.

I use the word 'sustainability' because its meaning is commonly understood but there are a couple of problems with the term as I see it. Firstly it seems to reinforce the world-view which treats the planet as a thing, more complex machine than biological being. We don't take care of our children because we want them to be more sustainable, to 'last longer' in pure resource terms, we do it because we want them to be healthy and happy. We do it out of love. The second issue I have with sustainability as a term, I have hinted at already: it seems to be more

---

[11] Thank you to Alastair Mackenzie and Monika Koncz Mackenzie

about making things last as long as possible, eking things out. That's what we do with supplies when we are worried they will run out, not how we treat a living, breathing being.

Regeneration, then offers a different image for our work of care and compassion for the planet. Living things regenerate and they do so only when they are healthy. If your body is well looked after, nourished with food, well rested and calm then your cells will naturally take care of themselves and regenerate when needed (within their natural capacity). We can view the planet in this way: as a being which, when taken good care of, will naturally regenerate. From this perspective our work in caring for the earth becomes relatively common-sense, even intuitive. This might seem like a kind of technical difference, an exercise in semantics, but what I suggest here is not just about the words, it is quite literally about a whole World-view. Do we see a complex but essentially mechanistic system made up of various 'resources' which we need to conserve, primarily to preserve ourselves, or do we see a huge living being which we can relate to with kindness and care. In the first instance we need experts to argue about and decide how best to conserve our limited resources, in the second we can orient ourselves around a simple question: how does this affect the planet? And how can we best care for the planet in this moment, in this act?

#

The mind-set I have talked about in that last section, where we see the planet as a complex set of resources to be managed and conserved, grows out of a particular assumption: That the planet or 'nature' is some kind of thing which exists 'over there' and we as human beings are separate from it. Generally speaking this separation is a kind of unconscious superiority complex which sets human beings as not just separate from, but better than, nature, having transcended it. We have become 'civilised.'

Not only does this assumption of separateness and superiority give birth to a profoundly unhealthy attitude towards the Earth, it is just inaccurate. We are not separate from nature, we are part of it. Some would argue a malfunctioning part of it, more like a virus, but part of it none-the-less. The sad irony is that many of the people who wish to conserve nature have this same underlying mind-set. So pervasive is this wonky cultural norm that even those who wish to care for the Earth look down on it. I have frequently come across a conversation amongst nature-loving people criticising buildings and cities and heavily underlining the distinction between 'man-made' and 'natural.' I can understand this, and in the past have been that voice of disdain for human-kinds' creations. The paradox that is usually missed here is that inherent within this dialogue is the same sense of separation between humans and nature which leads to treating it as a cache of resources to be used - and eventually used up.

If we are to truly heal the planet I think we must necessarily heal our relationship with the planet and that begins by relinquishing our sense of superiority and haughty transcendence. Once we do that we open the door to healing our deepest wound - that of separation. In separating ourselves from the being which gives us life, we cut ourselves off from the greatest source of wisdom for how to survive as a species and our greatest form of nourishment - not just for our bodies but for our psyches and our souls.

#

What all that I have said so far in this section points us towards is a deep need to relate to the planet Earth, the world around us, present in every moment, as a living being. We cannot continue making this planet, our home into an illegitimate object; good only to be used and, if we are lucky, left behind when we fly off to live on another planet. It is my contention that if we could make the collective cultural shift in world-view then our choices become clearer. When we see the planet as a legitimate other then complex questions about which resource is more vital to our survival and how we can be more clever, more frugal, or if a course of action will be more destructive, become much simpler questions. We can turn to the planet with compassion and ask what we might ask any being we met, and wished to support: What do you need right now? What do you need to thrive, long term? How can we help? The planet doesn't need to answer in words, when we see clearly enough from this perspective of caring for a being, I think what needs doing will be abundantly clear. I don't want to seem like I am over-simplifying this, in the broader sweeps of political and cultural policy more complex issues will likely take some big thinking from deep experts. However, even those experts will need to transform their way of seeing and relating to the world and in a grass-roots movement that begins in all of our everyday lives, I think many of the things we need to do are not so hard to spot. We must first see the planet as a legitimate being, and then we must find it in ourselves to act with compassion.

This is the core of why I call this book and this way of being 'Radical Embrace' - it is about embracing ourselves, deep at our core, embracing our bodies as integrated parts of our being, embracing each other regardless of affiliation, and embracing the planet as one of us: a being in need of love and care no less than the rest of us.

The world may need many voices and approaches - loud, public, skilful, legal, political voices for change - but if we can create within us a profound enough re-orientation of our attitude towards self, other, and world then that can be the personal radical act which ushers in profound societal change. As my friend Andy Bradley sometimes says:

"Learn how to <u>be</u> and you will know what to <u>do</u>."

So, as the fourth question, I'll ask you:

What kind of world do you want to leave behind you?

6

CONCLUSION:

DIALOGUE + ACTION

It is my belief and experience that conversations can change the world. And... if all that springs from this book is some comforting conversations then, while that would be a wonderful thing to have engendered in what can be a frightening world, it's not enough. Stuart Hill wrote:

"... my analysis of the situation is primarily psychosocial, rather than just political and that is exactly what makes such a proposition so difficult to accept, because for me this requires that I first recognise and act on my responsibilities and change myself before pointing fingers at others, or at least while concurrently doing this. This is not to deny the inequities and oppressions that exist and that need to be addressed within our societies, but rather to acknowledge that each of these can be traced to collective and individual patterns of behaviour, which if not changed will continue to wreak havoc with our precious planet, our societies and our individual well-being. Furthermore, I believe that the more empowered, aware, informed, competent and clear about our values that each of us is, then the more effective we are likely to be in bringing about the structural and institutional changes that are required. Trying to do the latter without addressing the former can only ever result in initiatives that will fail to address the causes of our problems and that at best can only slightly reduce the levels of unsustainability and degradation." [12]

---

[12] S. Hill, "Redesigning Agroecosystems for Environmental Sustainability: A Deep Systems Approach", in 'System Research and Behavioural Science' no. 15, John Wiley and Sons 1998

Even deep personal transformation is not enough though. I think it has to be part of any work we do to reclaim, nurture, and embrace our world but as I spoke of in chapter 1, I'm not a monk. I live in the mess and muddle of everyday life and I want to affect change there. My intention with this work is to help you to pick your battles. Whenever I look at the world I see so many causes crying for my attention that I end up feeling helpless and overwhelmed and I think a lot of other people do too. I simply can't respond to all the world's needs. But I have found that by asking myself the questions I have offered here, I have been able to connect with what I am most aligned to in terms of my values, beliefs, and sheer capacity so that I can at least throw my weight behind *something* that I believe to be constructive in creating a better world; a world I can feel proud to have been involved in creating for my son and all the children of Mother Earth.

To link the 4 core questions together, I'll offer another question. In some ways it is a short-cut to the others. I regularly ask myself this question and then seek to 'live into' (because it isn't always possible to conclusively answer the BIG questions):

What am I for?

This question operates at two levels. Firstly in terms of purpose - if I am a tool in the hands of the universe then what purpose do I serve. Having a powerful sense of purpose helps us to be resilient in the face of life's difficulties as well as helping us to know where to focus our action. Secondly in terms of being 'for' rather than 'against.' If it works for you, we need people to fight *against* the big inequalities, but I have found that I can find greater capacity to create positive change when I focus on what I want to create rather than what I want to destroy. Perhaps we can create and replace rather than destroy and rebuild.

If I know what I am for then the rest of the questions flow naturally out of this knowing:

- How do I put my leadership in service of it?
- How do I put more of it into the world in every moment by the stance I take?
- How do I engender more of it through my relationships?
- How do I create a lasting impact in the world in service to this purpose (a legacy)?

So I invite you to find your purpose for the greater good. Create dialogue, 'live into' the enquiry, and find allies to help you take action:

RADICAL EMBRACE

THE WORLD NEEDS WHAT YOU HAVE TO OFFER

RADICAL EMBRACE

RESOURCES

If you feel passionately about what I have explored in this book then a way that you can contribute to creating a better world is, as well as doing your own reflection and finding your own mission, to help others to find theirs. By forming communities of dialogue you may find allies to help you in your work either directly with the causes you most care about or more indirectly as companions on the path of making a difference. One way to form and gather these communities is to set up dialogue events where you can explore the questions I have offered here so you evoke a shared sense of passion and agency in the face of these challenging times. There is a short course I am preparing on Udemy.com to help you to lead these dialogues as elegantly and powerfully as possible. If you look the course up on Udemy it will be ready soon after publication of the book and you can use the coupon code "ihavethebook" to access the course for free.

The heart of this work, however, is making space to really hear each other as you reflect on and 'think out loud' about the questions I have offered. If you want to dive in to being in dialogue, in listening to each other, I would invite you to heed the advice William Isaacs shares in his wonderful book on dialogue:

"The Dark Side of Listening

For all the wonderful qualities of listening and the fully engaged participation that can be evoked through it, there is also an underside to this practice. As mentioned before, we tend to think in ways that lead us away from wholeness and into fragmentation. Again, fragmented listening is an abstraction, which literally means "extracting meaning from something." A part of me can listen and be fully participative while another part can abstract and fail to attend to what I hear - or attend only selectively. It is only by becoming aware of those parts of ourselves that fail to listen, even as we try hard to listen well, that we may breakthrough to a new experience.

A part of me can, in other words, remain high on the ladder of inference, and so have perceptions not grounded in directly observable experience. Instead of listening without resistance, I listen but resist what I hear, selecting what I want and discounting what I do not want to hear. When we have an axe to grind with someone, we tend to hear the grinding of the axes, not what the other person has to say.

Instead of allowing the quality of stillness to pervade our listening, it is easy to be in motion, seeking to "grasp" or "take in" what is being said. Our listening becomes more intellectual. We are "here," others are "there." We try to "get" what they say. Our thought is doing the interpreting. We are separate from the person, and then the "transmission" model of listening prevails. Have I received from them what I needed to perceive rather than what they were actually saying? Listening in this sense objectifies the other person. It is possible to listen in this way but we end up treating the other person as an object to manage not a being with whom we can create new possibilities.

What are we to do? The challenge is to become aware of the fact that especially when we try hard to listen, we will often still have a part of us actively failing to do so. The key is to simply become aware of this, to make conscious just what we are doing. Awareness is curative; as we stand still, our listening can open us into frontiers we did not realise were there."[13]

For ease of reference in reflecting on what I have offered in this book, here are the 4 key questions I offer at the end of each chapter along with the 5th meta-question:

---

[13] William Isaacs, "Dialogue and the Art of Thinking Together – A Pioneering Approach to Communicating in Business and in Life." Chapter 4, pages 108-109

For the sake of what will you embrace your power to lead?

What are you creating, each moment, through your presence?

What is the impact you are making on the lives of those around you?

What kind of world do you want to leave behind you?

RADICAL EMBRACE

What am I for?

OTHER READING & EXPLORATION

I have several other books out, a number of which touch on subjects which support this work. My next one, Cultivating Wisdom, will be especially relevant. I also have an **online programme** on Udemy.com, **'Warrior Leadership'** which connects directly with this programme.

There are many others doing great work and writing or teaching programmes around the themes of this book. A few that I am aware of and particularly admire are:

- Leadership:
    - Synchronicity – The Inner Path of Leadership by Joseph Jaworski
    - Conscious Business by Fred Kofman. There are also many free resources from him on the internet
    - Leaders and Misleaders by Andre Van Heerden
- Embodiment:
    - Mark Walsh's 'The Body of Leadership' online programme, he has a book coming soon too
    - Embodied Peacemaking by Paul Linden
    - Leadership Embodiment byWendy Palmer
    - The work of Dylan Newcombe (Uzazu)

- Compassion:
    - Mindful Compassion by Paul Gilbert
    - Andy Bradley's TEDx talk and other resources
    - Altruism: The Power of Compassion to Change Yourself and the World by Matthieu Ricard
- Sustainability/Regeneration:
    - Polly Higgins' books, talks and workshops
    - The 'Village Builders' online course from Jon Young (8 Shields)
    - The Nature Principle by Richard Louv
    - The work of Joanna Macy (The Work That Reconnects)
    - Permaculture: Principles and Pathways Beyond Sustainability by David Holmgren

AKNOWLEDGEMENTS

Without being too grand I do have some people to thank in this book. First of all is always my wife and son for being with me through the eccentric life I have chosen for myself and inflict on them – thank you for your patience and faith, I love you.

Several people have read the book pre-publication and offered me reflections, input or reviews. I am hugely grateful to you all for your time and care: Tom Kenward, Polly Higgins, Andy Bradley, Alastair Mackenzie, Monika Koncz-Mackenzie. Thank you.

Many teachers and colleagues have influenced me deeply over the years but for the work of this book Simon Buxton of The Sacred Trust, Sensei Steve Rowe of Shi Kon, Paul Linden of Being in Movement, Lance Giroux of The Samurai Game, Mark Walsh of Integration Training and Andy Bradley have been particularly influential. Thank you all.

There are many other teachers and companions on the path. In no particular order: Syd, Alan, Robbie, Niamh, Alex, Trish, Kate, Kate, Jamie, Claire, Clare, Tess, Dr. Adrian, Leanne, Judy, Ed, Rachel and many others! Thanks ☺ With Love.

ABOUT THE AUTHOR

Francis Briers has been exploring the mind-body connection and wisdom traditions for 20 years and facilitating learning for groups and individuals for 15.

He trained originally as an actor but then ran away from the circus to find his home. Along the way he studied martial arts (to black belt and instructor standard), Taoism, shamanism, bodywork, various spiritual and wisdom traditions from around the world, and was ordained as an Interfaith Minister and spiritual counsellor. He is a writer, facilitator, consultant and coach working with embodiment, conscious leadership, compassion and sustainability with organisations. He runs public workshops and online trainings on personal and spiritual development.

He lives in East Grinstead, UK, with his beloved and beautiful wife and son. He likes chocolate, sitting around fires, and being by the sea when it's stormy.

www.francisbriers.com

Enjoyed this book?

Tell your friends!

I'd love it, and it would really help me, if you could leave a review on Amazon – even a few words help make the work more visible.

Check out my website and sign up for my newsletter to get access to members' resources and hear about future books and online courses as soon as I create them:

www.fudoshin.org.uk/newsletter

Printed in Poland
by Amazon Fulfillment
Poland Sp. z o.o., Wrocław